WHAT WOULD UNICORN DO?

Magical Rules for a Happy Life

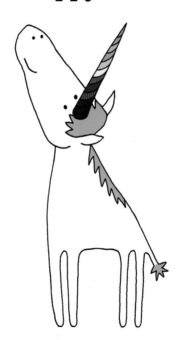

WHAT WOULD UNICORN DO?

Magical Rules for a Happy Life

SARAH FORD

ILLUSTRATED BY
ANITA MANGAN

spruce

FOR SARA

Unicorn has never been afraid of making decisions. Sometimes he follows his head and sometimes he follows his heart, but he always ends up on the right path – any wrong turns are just lessons learned. And he doesn't waste time worrying; what has happened in the past has gone, and who knows what might happen in the future. So 'live for the day' is definitely Unicorn's motto and the very reason why all around him ask themselves, 'What would Unicorn do?' whenever they are trying to decide on the right path or they are faced with a dilemma.

To be truly happy, Unicorn knows that his life has to have purpose, meaningful activities, happy relationships and a career that makes work not seem like work at all. Unicorn knows the value of downtime – pottering by himself at home, tending to the orchids, chilling out with a good book or dancing in the kitchen to a top tune – but then he also knows that there are times to get out and explore the big wide world, enjoy the company of fellow unicorns, breathe in the fresh air and listen to the birds sing. Variety is the spice of life for Unicorn, and he knows that there is beauty and inspiration all around, if you only choose to see it. Unicorn makes every moment count, because he knows that life is precious.

Unicorn is interested in people and not things. He is the friend that everyone loves, someone who will always invite you in for a coffee, pull up a comfy chair and offer a listening ear or a shoulder to cry on. To make the world a happier place, Unicorn tries to spread a little daily kindness; he is free with his hugs and his compliments, and he is a great inspiration for how to live well.

So take a leaf out of Unicorn's book – luckily, you happen to be holding a copy in your hands – and next time you're faced with a tricky situation, take a deep breath and ask yourself, 'What would Unicorn do?'

Unicorn would reach for the stars.

Unicorn would have
an open-door policy.

Unicorn would keep
a sense of wonder.

Unicorn would try
walking in someone
else's shoes.

Unicorn would
be modest.

Unicorn would go
the extra mile.

Unicorn would show love.

Unicorn would
always embrace
new things – even
beetroot juice.

Unicorn would enjoy
the smell of freshly
cut grass.

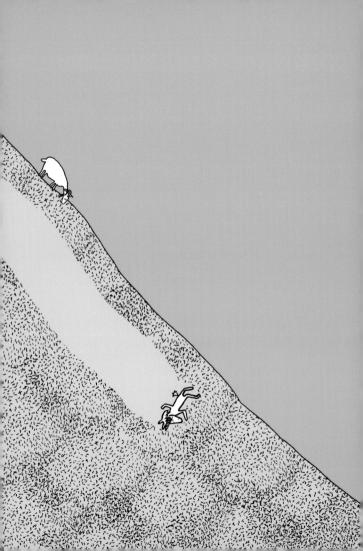

Unicorn would try
every ice-cream
flavour.

Unicorn would buy local.

Unicorn would wear
the sweater his
granny knitted.

Unicorn would try
his hoof at guerrilla
gardening.

Unicorn would
break the rules for
the greater good.

On hot days, Unicorn
would always wear his
hat and factor 30.

Unicorn would give
a little prod to get
things moving.

Unicorn would indulge
in Hollywood glamour.

Unicorn would wear
his lucky underwear.

Unicorn would put the
roof down.

Unicorn would always
be the first and last on
the dance floor.

Unicorn would look
after the planet.

Unicorn would jump
for joy.

Unicorn would always be proud to have friends in all colours and sizes.

Of course, Unicorn
would eat the cake
(just not all of it).

Unicorn would
know that muddy
knees = a good day.

Unicorn would
get back up.

Unicorn would be kind.

Unicorn would embrace
change.

Unicorn would
always remember
to floss.

Unicorn would put on
a brave face.

Unicorn would
have an open mind
about all things.

Unicorn would learn
from his elders.

Unicorn would only ever
be sad for a little while.

Unicorn would always look for the next challenge.

Unicorn would enjoy making everything just a bit more beautiful.

Unicorn would know
that more stuff =
more stuff to dust.

Unicorn would have
a rainy-day fund.

Unicorn would make
every day count.

Unicorn would keep
it simple.

Unicorn would know
when to keep quiet.

Unicorn would live in
the moment.

Unicorn would do something that scared him every day.

Unicorn would correct
a mistake.

So if you're ever stuck
and need some advice,
just ask yourself, what
would Unicorn do?

10 THINGS
THAT UNICORN
WOULD DEFINITELY
NOT DO
(NO THANK YOU, MA'AM):

- Stick his head out of the window of a moving train.
- Cry over spilled milk (though he might if it was gin).
- Worry about a bit of dust.
- Steal someone else's thunder.
- Be the first to say goodbye – you say it!
- Take himself too seriously.
- Dwell on the past – no way, José!
- Trample on others.
- Eat someone else's chocolate.
- Save things for best – every day is special.

An Hachette UK Company
www.hachette.co.uk

First published in Great Britain in
2018 by Spruce, a division of
Octopus Publishing Group Ltd
Carmelite House
50 Victoria Embankment
London EC4Y 0DZ
www.octopusbooks.co.uk

Distributed in the US by
Hachette Book Group
1290 Avenue of the Americas
4th and 5th Floors
New York, NY 10104

Distributed in Canada by
Canadian Manda Group
664 Annette St.
Toronto, Ontario, Canada M6S 2C8

ISBN 978-1-84601-566-3

A CIP catalogue record for this
book is available from the British
Library.

Printed and bound in China

10 9 8 7 6 5 4 3 2

Commissioning Editor
Sarah Ford
Assistant Editor
Ellie Corbett
Designer and Illustrator
Anita Mangan
Design Assistant
Robyn Shiner
Senior Designer
Jaz Bahra
Production Controller
Sarah Kulasek-Boyd